It was May 15th. We were on a walk in the foothills of the Chugach Mountains near Anchorage, Alaska. Perhaps due to the late spring, I wasn't thinking much about moose calves until we rounded a corner on the trail in time to witness a mother giving birth to the second of twins. I've seen lots of moose, but I never expected to witness a birth! I returned several times over the next few days and throughout the eventual record late-season snow, wondering how the young moose could possibly survive. The result is this book, a true story, straight from the heart of nature.

Funding for the first printing of *Moose in May* was accomplished through kickstarter.com, a website that helps fund creative projects. Thanks to all who supported our book, especially:

Bruce and Gayle Walker	Amy and Carlos Huddleston
Bob and Debra Burgelin	John Dwyer
Shannon Brown	Susan Hviid
Lennie Higgins	Zach and Nancy Kozicki
Rick Skinner	Chris and Amy Reed

For children of all ages

©2014 by John Schwieder and Cindy Kumle
Edited by Sue Mitchell, Inkworks
All rights reserved. No portion of this book may be reproduced, stored, or transmitted in any form.
No part of this book may be sold individually.
ISBN: 978-0-9794874-3-9
Printed in China
First Printing 2014

Published by John Schwieder, Photographer
Anchorage, Alaska
www.johnschwieder.com
john@johnschwieder.com
Books and photographs available from the author.

For those who protect and love wild places.

Every year starting in mid-May,
just as winter is ending
and summer has begun,
moose seek a quiet, protected place
in the woods to have their babies.

The days are getting longer.
The snow has melted.
The land is warmer
and greener every day.

This mother moose is searching for the
perfect spot to give birth.

But this will not be an ordinary spring for
her or her calves.

She has found a secluded knoll with a view all around.

Her calf has been born.

Mom tends to her new baby.

There's a second calf.

It's twins!

Before long the calves discover each other.

Moose usually have one or two calves and rarely triplets.

From 20% up to 70% of moose have twins. The likelihood of twins is greater when mom has plenty of food.

Moms and calves use scent to recognize each other.

The second calf is already trying to stand.

He is just a half-hour old.

Those new legs are wobbly!

The first twin is a girl.

She is smaller, more compact,
but still has long moose legs!

The second twin is a boy.

When males are fully grown they are bigger than females.

His body is already longer.

Newborn twins weigh 15 to 18 pounds. A single calf is heavier, weighing 28 to 35 pounds.

A fully grown male moose can weigh more than 1,600 pounds, a female 1,200. They are 5 to 6 1/2 feet tall at the shoulder. Only males have antlers.

Now both calves are testing their legs.

Mom keeps a watchful eye.

It's getting dark and time to leave the moose for the night.

Calves stand within a few minutes of birth and outrun a human in just a few days. Adult moose run 35 mph and swim 6 mph.

Mom's main job is to be on lookout for danger. Large ears gather sound and can be aimed in different directions. Eyes have few detectors for color but many for black and white, which helps them see in twilight. The large nose is 200 times more sensitive than a human's and four times more than a dog's.

The second morning finds
the moose still on the knoll.

The calves are already tall enough
to nurse while standing up.

There is a chill in the air.

It feels like a change in the weather.

Moose milk is very nutritious; it is twice as concentrated as cow milk. Calves drink up to two liters per day and gain two pounds per day for the first month.

Calves start eating vegetation in about one month, but keep nursing for four or five months.

It's the middle of May.

All the snow had melted.

Now, new snowflakes begin to fall.

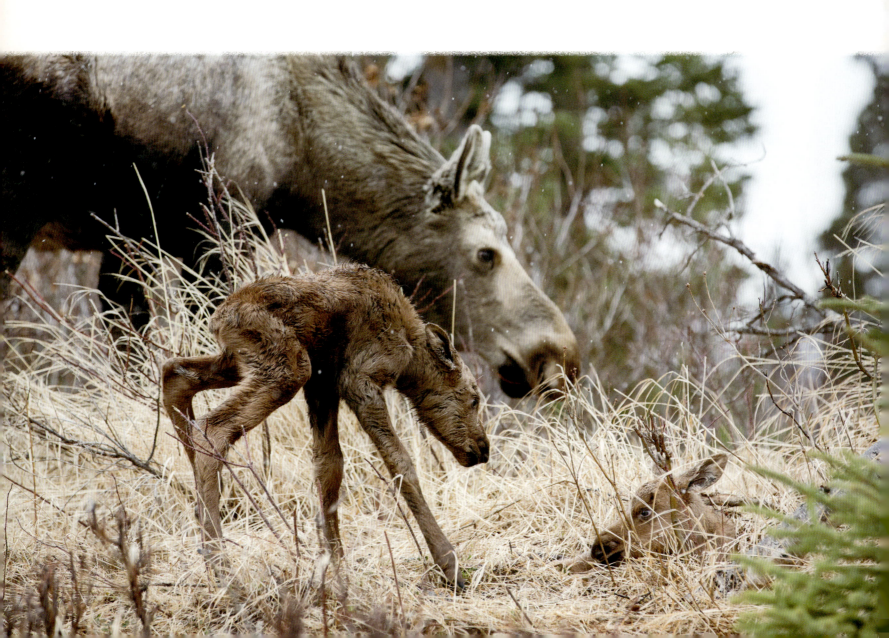

Clouds are descending.

Snow is swirling all around.

A storm has arrived.

All moose calves are born over a short period of about three weeks from mid-May to early June. This gives young moose an early start so they can grow over the warm, abundant summer months and be prepared to survive their first winter.

These calves were born May 15, early in what would turn out to be a record cold and snowy spring.

It's snowing one minute,
then raining the next.

The moose are getting soaked!

For the first week, moose stay within 150 feet of the birth site. They will remain in the area for at least a month.

Even as adults, the calves may not stray too far from their mother's territory.

Even in the storm,
the calves start to explore.

They leave the knoll,
disappearing over the hill for the night.

On day three,
the moose are surrounded
by snow!

Mom is easy to see.

Can you find the babies?

A new cold record for May 17 was set this day, shattering the previous record low temperature by 7 degrees.

It was also a record snowfall day, with a storm total of about 7 inches in the area.

The 2012-2013 snow season was 232 days, the longest ever recorded.

The calves look cold.

**Can you imagine,
two days old,
stuck out in a blizzard?**

It's a good sign that they are still feeding...

and curious about all the snow.

Eating and activity are what keeps all creatures warm.

Although adult moose are well adapted for cold and snow, calves don't normally encounter snowstorms for at least five months.

On day four
the snowfall has stopped
and it's looking brighter.

The moose have found shelter
under trees, where they
have dried off a little.

Alert moose ears seem to say all is okay.

Moose maintain a body temperature of 101 to 102 degrees,
2 to 3 degrees warmer than humans.

Before long mom is on the move, looking for something to eat.

The bond between a mother moose and her calves is strong. Instinctively, calves know to stay close for protection and learning.

The calves learn everything about their new world by watching mom.

Moose are plant eaters.

In spring they eat twigs and new leaf buds —when they can find them!

Their favorite food is willow shrubs.

Moose are herbivores. They mostly eat twigs and leaves of woody plants, favoring willow, birch, and aspen. They also eat sedges, forbs (herbs), horsetail, and vegetation from shallow ponds.

Young moose learn to eat by imitating their mother's choices. They may start nibbling on vegetation when only a few days old.

The sun is shining on day five.

The snow is melting.

Spring is a brown and white world and the moose blend into their surroundings.

Can you find all three?

Moose live in northern forests with protected areas. They are found along rivers, in freshwater marshes, ponds, willow thickets, and on timberline plateaus.

The calves are venturing farther from mom but not from each other!

Can you tell which one is the brother and which is the sister?

Moose color ranges from golden brown to almost black. The hair of newborn calves is red-brown, fading to a lighter rust color within a few weeks. By late summer, calves have shed their rust-colored coat and replaced it with hair that is similar in texture and color to that of adults.

Long legs and a long nose help moose reach high branches.

They eat about fifty pounds of plants every day.

Moose have no upper front teeth. They do have a very sensitive upper lip that can distinguish between fresh shoots and harder twigs. The lip can grasp and strip an entire branch of leaves in a single mouthful.

The name moose comes from Algonquian, a native American language, meaning "he strips off": a reference to the way moose strip leaves from a tree as they eat.

The moose are moving more each day.

The twins may still be little,
but long legs help them keep up.

Moose may move seasonally to calving, mating, and wintering areas. They travel anywhere from only a few miles to as many as sixty.

Moose move individually, not as a group or herd like caribou.

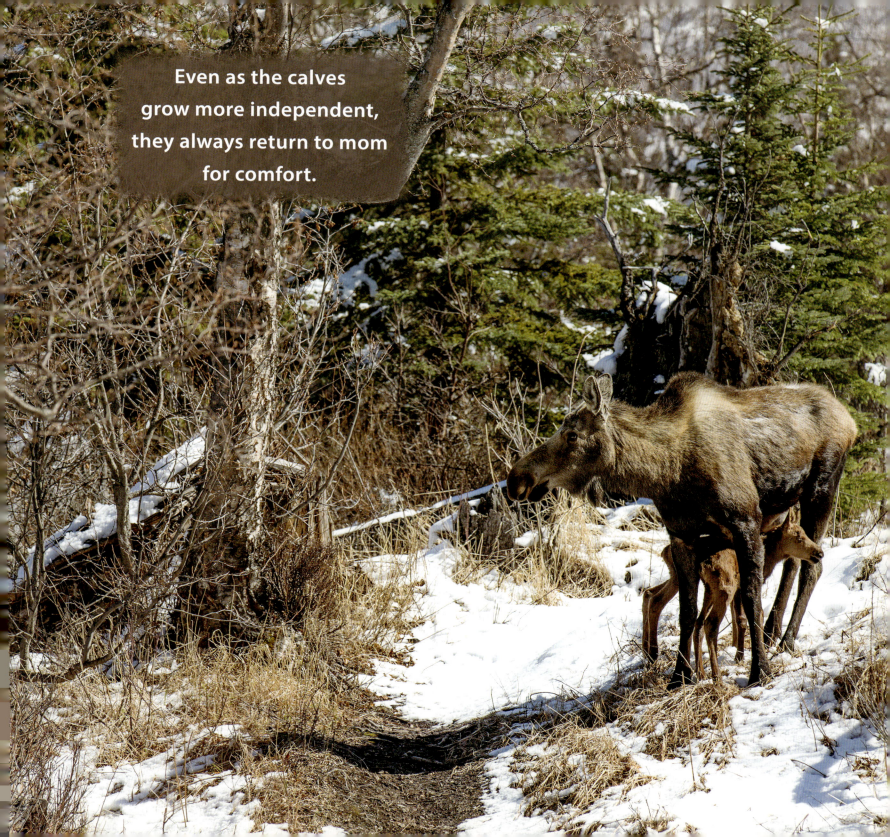

Even as the calves grow more independent, they always return to mom for comfort.

Summer is a time of abundance for moose. They feed up to twelve hours per day, mostly on green, new plants, increasing their body weight. Their dark coat absorbs heat from sunshine but can lead to overheating in summer.

Moose do have adaptations to help survive winter. Their fur is thicker. Their large, rectangular shape minimizes heat loss. Still, winter can be a difficult time. Snow makes it harder to get to food. Moose reduce activity, resting much of the day. Feeding time decreases to about six hours on twigs, branches, and bark.

A moose might lose up to 35% of its body weight in winter.

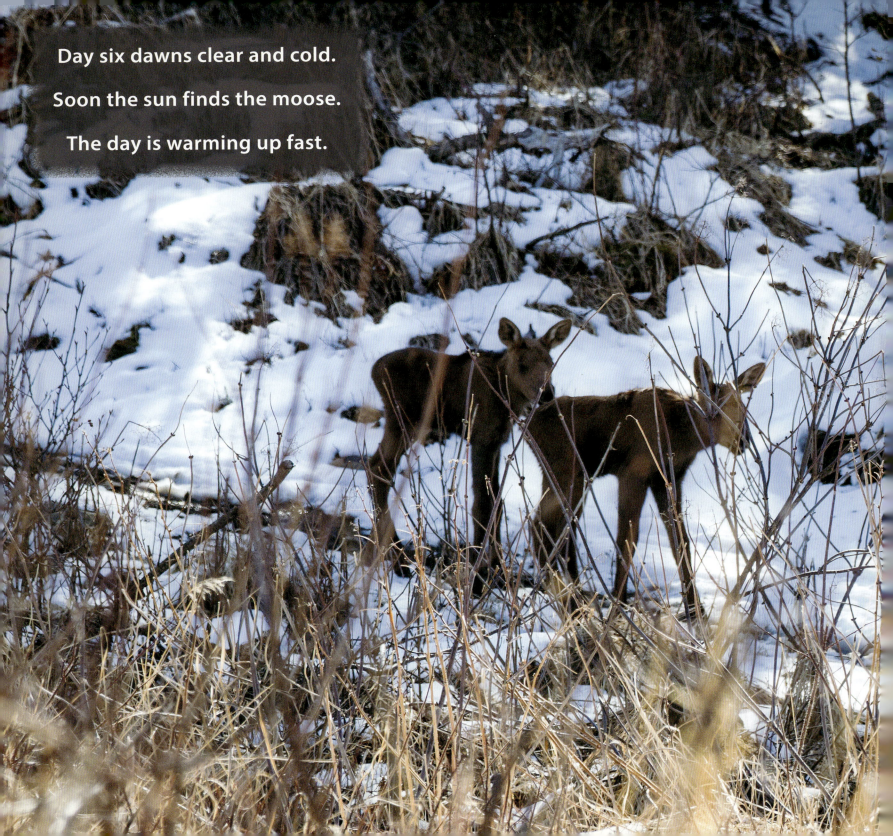

Day six dawns clear and cold.

Soon the sun finds the moose.

The day is warming up fast.

Long legs and broad hooves help moose travel in dense forest, marshy areas, through lakes and ponds, and through soft snow. Deep snow is difficult or impossible to move in, and snow crust will cause moose to restrict their movements or seek more sheltered terrain.

By evening the snow is almost gone.

Mom is always watching out for danger.

Her main job is keeping the calves safe.

A mother moose can be fiercely protective when faced with any perceived threat. Unlike other members of the deer family, moose mothers do not hide their offspring. They stand and fight. Moose have sharp hooves and can strike with precision, using both front and back feet. Never approach a mother moose too closely!

It's day seven.

The calves are one week old!

They have survived
their first storm.

Now they can look forward
to a summer of growing.

By fall they will weigh
300 pounds!

Moose grow faster than any other land-based animal, as much as four pounds per day. By fall the calves will be ten times heavier than their birth weight. They will stop growing over their first winter and start again the next spring.

The twins will stay together with mom for one year, discovering everything a young moose needs to know.

A mother moose will chase her yearlings off just before giving birth the next spring. Calves may stay near for months, eventually finding their own territory.

Wow, what a first week for the calves!

By the time the snow falls again, they will be ready.

How wonderful it was that we could share their epic beginning!

THE END